W9-BBY-953

flowers *for the* table

flowers *for the* table

ARRANGEMENTS AND BOUQUETS
FOR ALL SEASONS

BY ARIELLA CHEZAR

TEXT BY ELISE CANNON

PHOTOGRAPHS BY
SHAUN SULLIVAN

CHRONICLE BOOKS
SAN FRANCISCO

Text copyright © 2002
by Ariella Chezar.
Photographs copyright
© 2002 by Shaun Sullivan.
All rights reserved.
No part of this book may
be reproduced in any form
without written permission
from the publisher.

Library of Congress
Cataloging-in-Publication
Data available.
ISBN: 0-8118-2965-0
Manufactured in China

Designed by Tamar Kondy

Distributed in Canada
by Raincoast Books
9050 Shaughnessy Street
Vancouver, British Columbia
V6P 6E5

10 9 8 7 6 5 4 3 2 1

Chronicle Books LLC
85 Second Street
San Francisco, California
94105

www.chroniclebooks.com

With all my love to Famke, Howard, Pamela, and Barbara:
it is because of you that I am

flowers *for the* table

preface

The principle I adhere to most in floral design is the basic "to every thing, there is a season." From childhood days in the garden, I learned that the life cycle of a plant has an apex, a moment where it shines in perfection. This is the moment I try to capture with my work. I start with the flower itself, the one that is freshest and most replete with life, and build around it.

As a girl who grew up in the Berkshires of Massachusetts, a place with pronounced seasonal changes, I was lucky enough to have many family rituals that were fashioned around specific times of year. In the fall, we made maple-leaf crowns. Winters were long and without much color unless we brought branches indoors and coaxed them into bloom. When spring rolled around, there were Easter-egg mobiles to make: blown goose, duck, and hen eggs that we would color and hand decorate using a wax-resist method, then hang with grapevines and ribbons. Another spring ritual I remember was daffodil-picking at an abandoned tennis court where the flowers spread like a golden coverlet. Then all summer long, we had our family garden to draw from. August usually sent us blueberry-picking with buckets and baskets, mouths full and fingers stained. Throughout the year, we wandered through fields and climbed trees, exploring the natural world and witnessing what each season has to offer.

My mother, an artist and avid gardener, taught me from my earliest days about the treasures of the natural world and about living things in their seasons. As I grew up, I studied drama, dance, and opera. The environment of the theater—the way music, costumes, lighting, and set design momentarily transport the audience—mesmerized me. Could I combine my enthusiasm for this kind of transformation with the natural world my mother had taught me to love so well? Luckily, I found Pamela Hardcastle and Barbara Bockbrader, two mentors who were garden and floral designers, who made me realize that I could do just that.

Pamela and Barbara showed me that art and life can be intertwined. Evidence of their creativity pervades every corner of their own gardens and homes. They taught me countless ways to change the space around us, utilizing nature's power. They taught me about color, form, and texture. From them, I learned that flowers are living, breathing entities that grace our world for small moments in time. With the ideas in this book, I hope to share this knowledge and passion with you, season by season.

introduction

flower arranging basics

LOOK TO THE FLOWER FOR INSPIRATION

Just as the best tomatoes and strawberries come in summer, one learns that the fullest tulips appear in spring. Garden roses are at their most fetching in May, June, and July. Knowing that lilacs will appear for only a few scant weeks has made more than one bride set her wedding date for that time, because she wants to recall their delicate scent on each anniversary. When I make floral arrangements for restaurants, I follow their lead in using only the day's freshest ingredients. I make no design decisions until I've entered the San Francisco Flower Mart (at 2:00 A.M. most days!) and carefully perused their selection of blooms for the perfect rose, tulip, or flowering branch. Perfect because it was picked at exactly the right time.

Choosing the freshest flowers is the key to beautiful arrangements—it's almost impossible to fail with the right flowers as your medium. The ideas below indicate how adhering to a few basics will influence you as you create your own bouquets, and throughout this book I'll return to them again and again.

- In their natural state, flowers are not usually packed together tightly, so try to make arrangements full but loose, with petals, leaves, and tendrils extending below and beyond their containers.

- So many flowers look perfectly stunning by themselves, without any addition whatsoever; add others only when you want to enhance specific colors and create different textures.

- Rather than mixing colors uniformly throughout a bouquet, make small clusters of each shade and place them alongside one another: the larger blocks of color will complement each other more fully.

- Use the flower's own leaves if they're long lasting or try to find greenery that has some resemblance to the flower's own, to echo its appearance in nature.

- Each addition to an arrangement should have a purpose. If you have only a few flowers, it's better to make an exquisite small bouquet rather than adding filler to make it look bigger.

- Don't cut flowers to fit a vase—instead, choose the vase that best suits the blossom.

Choosing the right container is important but relatively easy if you do so based on the size and criteria of the bouquet itself. Anything that holds water can be used as a vessel for flowers, as you'll see in the section on containers (page 18), which discusses how to expand your vase collection in unusual ways. Also presented in this book are uses for fabric, ribbons, and other fanciful additions.

As you look through these pages, consider the spirit of the arrangements and regard them as departure points for projects that reflect your own style. Each seasonal section offers a variety of design schemes: riotous color and understated monochromatic palettes; profuse bouquets and simple posies; assemblages that incorporate not only flowers but also fruits, berries, and even vegetables. Flowers are naturally gorgeous—if you work with their lines and shapes, not against them, your results will look uncontrived, and therefore beautiful.

FINDING, CONDITIONING, AND HANDLING FLOWERS

Basic Supplies

Most arrangements in this book can be made with clippers, a sharp knife, and a pair of garden gloves. For more complicated work, you may need a thorn stripper, floral tape, floral clay, wire, and metal flower-arranging frogs. All of these are available at floral supply stores and some craft and hardware stores. Keep bleach and sponges on hand for cleaning vases; a bottle brush is good for narrow-necked containers. Some projects call for scissors, a hot-glue gun, craft glue, a sponge brush for applying glue, fabric, ribbon, and fine clear or iridescent glitter. A cache of strong rubber bands is also useful.

Most of the flower and plant varieties mentioned in this book will be available from your local florist. Consider asking them to include your favorites in their weekly order. Farmers' markets and nurseries are good sources for unusual cuttings and other surprises. If you cannot locate specific flowers, don't give up hope. With an adventurous spirit and an eye toward the overall effect, you'll be able to come up with a satisfying substitute. Remember, the fresher the better!

While many consider conditioning flowers and greenery a chore, it is necessary and can be a satisfying experience if you do two things: allow yourself plenty of time (like most creative activities, it always takes longer than you think it will) and make your work space as organized and comfortable as possible. A good chair, pleasant conversation or music, and comfortable clothes truly make all the difference.

STEP ONE

Scrub all glass and ceramic containers with bleach, as soap residue is harmful to some flowers. Bleach also keeps the water free of bacteria. After cleaning clear containers, polish them with a soft cloth to get rid of marks and smudges.

STEP TWO

The most important step in preparing flowers is to assure that their stems can take in water easily. Without hydration, a stem will dry out and lose its ability to drink in a very short period.

- Recut stems as soon as you bring flowers home, again when you begin arranging them, and again a few days later if possible.

- Cut all flower stems at an angle with your clippers or a sharp knife. (For safety, use clippers for all thick or woody stems.) This not only creates a larger surface area for hydration, it also keeps stems pressed against a vase bottom from becoming blocked.

- Unless you know exactly how tall you want the final arrangement to be, leave enough stem so that you can experiment with height while making the bouquet itself.

- Branches or woody stems should be split and crosscut at the bottom to allow for more water intake. (Note: smashing branch ends with a hammer achieves the same purpose but can make the water dirty.)

- When preparing irises, tulips, daffodils, hyacinths, and other flowers that come from bulbs, be sure to cut off the hard white section at the bottom of the stem so that water can be more readily absorbed. Place in cold water after cutting.

- Cut away all excess foliage. Leaves often suck away water, so unless they will be featured in your work, it's best to strip them away while the flowers acclimatize. Likewise, remove all leaves that may fall below the water level so that they do not decay and soil the water.

- Changing the water every few days also helps prolong a blossom's life.

STEP THREE

Further prepare your flowers and greenery so that they will be perfectly ready when you begin your work.

- Sometimes it may be necessary to pick off buds that detract from the simplicity of a single bloom.

- To remove dust and pests from leaves, ferns, or other gathered foliage that you plan to feature, swish them in warm water and dry them lightly with a soft cloth.

- After performing these basics, let the flowers rest awhile in a cool spot. It can take a few hours for them to adjust to their surroundings.

- Waiting overnight before assembling can force buds to open, revealing hidden interior colors and details.

Start arranging! Following are some general tips for handling flowers.

- Position each flower individually, adjusting lengths as necessary.

- Some buds can be coaxed open in warm rooms, or by hand, as with poppies. By carefully peeling away the protective pods from the bottom, you can gently release the petals.

- Outer petals can also be manipulated on lilies, and the papery sheaths can be pulled away from daffodils and other narcissus to speed their opening.

- If you're not achieving the effect you'd like immediately, have patience. This stage should be a relaxing one for you and the flower, so take your time and let the beauty of the blossom do most of the work.

- Don't crush blooms into vases. If you need to rearrange or pull them up over the vase rim, use both hands and gently lift the blossoms from below and let their heads rest outside the container.

Most people who don't work directly with flowers don't realize that each individual stem has been prepared and hand placed into the final product, often with painstaking care. This is where your artistry and passion for the work comes in. So just take your time, judge your efforts kindly, and watch your skills blossom.

CONTAINERS

It's incredibly satisfying to stand back and look at beautiful freshly cut flowers after placing them in the perfect container, the one most suited to their shape and height. The vases that most florists' arrangements come in are so tall and narrow that they can't be used for many types of flowers. To find a variety of shapes and sizes, especially smaller, wider styles, I have made it a goal to seek out one new, inexpensive vessel at every garage sale or flea market I go to—as a result, I've discovered lots of great substitutes for what is traditionally called a vase. See what you can find at antique shops, secondhand stores, and even the back of your own kitchen cupboard. Here are some general guidelines:

- For a homey or country look, try items like enameled coffeepots, ceramic teapots and cups, sugar bowls, creamers, and water pitchers.

- Glassware—like shot glasses, Moroccan tea glasses, champagne flutes, parfait glasses, water goblets, pint glasses, and almost any fancy dessert container— looks pretty with flexible stems and blossoms spilling over the lip. Keep a few glasses by the sink or worktable for buds that break off larger arrangements or plant snippets that might take root in water.

- Clear glass is best for spring flowers like tulips, narcissus, and daffodils, as their stems are such a fresh shade of green they should be shown off. Make sure to gently clean between leaf and stem where soil and sand become trapped.

- Silver or pewter tea services, with their pots, creamers, and sugar bowls, make great containers for a table featuring a large arrangement and two satellites.

- Other silver pieces I pounce on at flea markets are bud vases, saltcellars, and toothpick holders. Sometimes, tiny posies at each place setting are so charming they can take the place of a central table arrangement.

- For field flowers and wild-looking bouquets, try vintage tins such as coffee cans, spice tins, olive oil kettles, baking soda and salt boxes, and metal canisters. If they're too rusty to hold water, line them with a plastic bag before filling. Some modern canned foods now have retro labels that achieve the same effect as the vintage ones. You can also peel away labels and use the shiny cylinders beneath.

- It's hard to resist old canning jars, perfume flasks, patent medicine vials, and blue and brown apothecary bottles. Every once in a while, their labels will still be attached, though tattered, a nice effect.

- Functional glassware such as beakers, storage jars, and flasks make striking, modernistic containers.

- For large arrangements with big branches, choose cylindrical galvanized pails, cast aluminum canisters, and, if you can find them, garden urns. These are often made of painted or rusted metal, terra-cotta, concrete, or stone. Tall, opaque containers can be weighted with stones or marbles to keep heavy branches from tipping them over.

- When arranging graceful stems like calla lilies, it's a shame to hide their stalks, so a tall, clear cylinder or ginger jar works well.

- Bowls, whether glass, silver, or ceramic, imply abundance. They are an obvious choice for fruits, vegetables, and berries. Certain types of leaves also look lovely in them, as well as floating roses or gardenias.

- Compotes are essentially bowls on pedestals. They lift the assemblage off the table without sacrificing the full, round effect of the arrangement as a tall, narrow container might.

The important thing to remember when choosing a container for your arrangement is that if it can hold water, it can hold flowers. I've cut more than one Evian bottle down to create a vessel that didn't detract at all from its breathtaking contents. By working on your vase collection and keeping a few choices at the ready, you begin to see which types of containers are best suited to certain flower qualities. If you let the flowers dictate your choice of container and not the other way around, you'll make some useful discoveries about both. Let the treasure hunt begin!

the promise *of* spring

"Pleasure," wrote Colette, "derives from what we have forgotten." Spring pushes up and out with all the force of new life, and with it comes the pleasure of remembering what is possible, ideas that winter may have numbed us into forgetting. In the dreary days of February, it's easy to think spring will never arrive—until one wet morning when bare branches have, literally overnight, transformed into blossoming trees. It seems a miracle when pink and cream puffs of apple, almond, and quince become suddenly, astonishingly abundant. Daffodils startle in the same way: one day green stems push up through the earth, and the next they're tossing blonde heads, demanding attention. It's almost as if the insistent new flowers propel us into action, into reentering the natural world. Or at least into inviting nature indoors again.

What comes first in spring, the desire to have parties or the flowers that beg to be celebrated? It may just be that a frilly bouquet of stunning parrot tulips inspires a spur-of-the-moment brunch. Or that the ephemeral quality of lilacs reminds us how important it is to seize the moment, gather friends, and improvise a birthday party in the hour it takes to bake a cake. For me, the spirit of the season takes over when I look outside and see that the earth is thawing. I pull out the seed catalogs and imagine planting new flowers and other plants in my garden. Spring is characterized by energy, freshness, and possibility.

With such a wealth of flowers blooming at this time, it's difficult to choose one over another: irises, narcissus, primroses, freesias, and many other beauties in colors and fragrances wake up the senses. No flower symbolizes spring's fresh beauty as boldly perhaps as the tulip, so I have incorporated several kinds into the following arrangements. I have also used turban ranunculus, a blossom so versatile and lush it's sometimes called "spring's rose." I have mixed traditional favorites with some lesser-used varieties, such as clematis, frittilaria, and hellebores, that are currently gaining popularity with growers and florists.

For a springtime brunch, ranunculus is combined with five-leaf akebia, checkered lily, and an unusual celadon green hellebore. A tea service filled with peach tulips and salmon ranunculuses strikes a whimsical note at an elegant dinner party, as does a cocktail glass filled with bright orange clivia. And in a season where it's easy to go wild with multicolored arrangements, a table filled with containers of cream, white, and pale pink varieties is cool and sophisticated, while a pure-white arrangement for an outdoor buffet reflects simplicity and plenitude at the same time.

Spring signifies not only the waking of the Earth's plants, but also the reawakening of our senses. With the colors, fragrances, textures, and flavors that we enjoy at this time of year, it's as if all of our cognitive powers are reborn. After a season of sleep, we experience the natural world once again, not just with our minds, but right down inside our bones.

garden *compote*

With spring's beauties bursting outdoors, why not echo that abundance by creating your own densely "planted" patch of blossoms inside? Close your eyes and think of spring—what colors come to mind? For me, fresh colors arise from childhood associations: Easter eggs, a favorite tablecloth of my mother's, and the first appearance of crocus. Whatever the reason, I envision plum, pale green, and white. This pure, sophisticated combination was my choice for the arrangement here, perfect for a brunch to celebrate the new season. You can create a similar bouquet using your own favorite spring colors.

Setting out with my own dream palette in mind for this arrangement, I wasn't sure what I'd come home with but I was delighted by the results. I found celadon green hellebore *(Helleborus foetidus)*, violet checkered lily *(Frittilaria meleagris)*, and plum and white ranunculus, as well as a plum-edged variety. Finally, a bit of five-leaf akebia with dusty plum-and-white flowers was a lucky last-minute find. Its offshoots resemble small butterflies floating above the flowers. Note how the pale jade compote lifts the arrangement up off the table so that all of its treasures can be more easily appreciated.

This kind of container requires the use of a frog, a heavy spiked anchor, concealed inside. If it has enough weight, the frog will stay put. If not, try affixing it with a small bit of floral clay. Fill the bowl with water. Start by positioning the woody vines of the akebia into the spikes of the frog. They should drape over the edge; where they're extra-long, consider twisting them back and dipping the ends into the bowl. Get comfortable with the twisting and doubling back of vines. Moving to the other stiff-stemmed flowers, place the hellebores into the frog, again with the goal of letting the clusters cascade over the edge. This should provide enough of a framework to allow you to place the ranunculuses and checkered lilies anywhere in the bowl with ease, as long as you ensure that they're able to reach the water.

If you've never used a compote for flower arranging before, you might want to seek one out. When you need a bouquet that rises above the table but you want to preserve the fullness and scale that a bowl provides, a compote is the perfect container. A tall vase might prove too vertical for short, plump flowers and trailing vines and could overwhelm the rest of the table. The compote's bowl allows flowers to relax into their natural postures. Ceramic, glass, pottery, pewter, and silver-plated versions can be found in department and housewares stores.

peach *profusion*

Because they are some of spring's earliest bloomers, I typically find myself making my first tulip purchase of the season on a damp, cold day.

Nothing cheers up a blustery March afternoon like a big bundle of bright peach tulips. Chilly, wet weather tempts me to create a cozy, glowing environment at home, and blossoms like these are certainly reason enough to throw a party. When it comes to varieties, I can't hide my enthusiasm for parrot tulips over almost any other kind. With their huge blooms, their striated petals, and the way their shapes change from day to day, they're so much more interesting and exotic to me than the basic oval-shaped tulip. It's almost as if they are two entirely different flowers. Some of the better known types are the 'Apricot Parrot,' used in the arrangements here; the 'Flaming Parrot', so called for its bright red and yellow striations; and the maroon-and-green 'Black Parrot'.

It's important to note that it may take some time for tulips to open fully, from a few hours to almost five days, depending on how closed they are when purchased. After you bring them indoors and recut the stems, place them in cold water. Then prepare to be dazzled. Tulips move and change and twirl as they adjust to their surroundings.

Often when you place them in water, they droop down for a day or so, then surprise you by standing straight up. They seem to have a mind of their own.

Graceful tulips can make even the simplest arrangements look elegant, and with its round head and whorled layers of petals, the ranunculus makes a perfect companion. It can be used like a rose, and some larger varieties have even been compared to peonies. Spring brings a profusion of ranunculuses into the markets, and florists

often use them at this time of year, not only for their beauty but also because they're usually inexpensive compared to tulips or hothouse roses. Like the tulip, the ranunculus is a bulb flower, along with the daffodil, crocus, gladiolus, freesia, and iris. All flowers that come from bulbs do best when placed in cold water after cutting.

The flowers themselves are the real stars of this dinner-party table. Other touches, like silver candle-sticks and pewter-edged plates, add to the effect. I put pieces of an old silver tea service into use as containers, along with a bud vase found at a garage sale. To emphasize luxuriance, make sure to give the buds plenty of time to open before arranging, so the ranunculuses are full and round and the tulips are at their frilliest.

The tulips have been cut fairly short so that their heads will droop all around the rim of the open teapot. Experiment by snipping bits of stem until you've got the length just right. Salmon and orange ranunculuses, with their firmer stems, are then used to fill in and shape the bouquet. The wide-open tulips in the bud vase have been cut as short as possible so that their heads can be fully supported and their centers visible. A creamer and sugar bowl are pretty vases for the smaller nosegays, which are made entirely of ranunculuses.

Because so few people have use for an old-fashioned tea service these days, you can purchase them fairly cheaply at flea markets and estate sales. While this one resembles pewter, it's actually a tarnished, almost black-ened, silver-plate that gleams and contrasts with the bright flowers. It's a good idea to put a few blossoms into your garage sale treasures and see how they look before you rush for the silver polish. It takes some time and diligence to amass a variety of vases, so fear not if you don't yet have your own tea set for this purpose. A few clear glass pieces, such as a selection of dessert glasses, could substitute gracefully here.

To add color and texture to the setting, we used ribbon in the arrangement. Fabric lends elegance to simple votive candles. For the bouquet embellishment, take a generous length of wide ribbon like this three-inch blue violet moiré and fold it in half. Twist at the center with wire; 22-gauge floral works well but any flexible wire will suffice. Take

the twisted end and push it deep into the container, then drape the ribbon to one side, cutting the ends at angles.

For the most romantic effect, light tapers above the arrangement and use smaller candles to illuminate the flowers from below. It's easy to make votive candles glow in different colors and patterns. Locate small, inexpensive glass holders at craft, floral supply, or home decorating stores. Wrap the containers with a few inches of fabric or ribbon and secure the ends with a seam of hot glue. Six or eight candles, randomly placed, will warm up the setting and intensify the blossoms' own colors.

If you are creating an arrangement for an event, remember that no matter how formal it may be, it's important to maintain a sense of playfulness. Pairing something whimsical like a teapot with fancy linens and delicate crystal demonstrates a light touch. If you go with your instincts and make the setting inviting but not fussy, the party will most likely follow suit, with easy conversation and warm, memorable moments.

springtime
w h i t e s

One of the miraculous things about fresh flowers is how they transform the spaces around them. When placed in front of a window like this, an arrangement can create a visual connection between the view outside and the interior of a home. By inviting nature indoors throughout the year, you can claim the world beyond your window, making it a part of your living space.

Some of the prettiest, palest flowers available are in this assemblage: snowdrop, anemone, clematis, ranunculus, eucharis (Amazon lily), and lily of the valley, along with a handful of creamy 'Manon Lescaut' daffodils. The vertical element of the display is created with blush-colored quince blossoms. Note that each arrangement holds only a single type of flower and that all bouquets are placed in clear containers so that the backlight shines through the glass. Surprisingly, though each element was simple and quickly done, the overall effect appears rather intricate.

There are world-famous floral designers who use a single color or even just a single variety of flower to achieve stunning effects at weddings and other gala events. By filling a space in an extremely unified way, the designer encourages the guests to more closely examine and truly appreciate the psychological power of one color or the intricate beauty of a single blossom. Some "powerhouse" flowers, such as 'Casablanca' lilies, virtually require this kind of showcase because they are so striking and fragrant, almost larger than life. They're like the divas of the plant kingdom. The truth is, almost any freshly cut flower looks gorgeous among its own kind. Whether in a Victorian silver urn or a simple jelly jar, an armful or a thimbleful, a dozen identical flowers can, when plucked at the right time, truly take your breath away.

venetian glass bouquet
and clivia cocktail

CLIVIA

POPPY

RANUNCULUS

PARROT TULIPS

CRÈME UPSTAR TULIPS

MAPLE FLOWER

CLEMATIS FOLIAGE

Asymmetry is an important component of natural-looking arrangements because it more closely resembles a garden setting. Don't be afraid to group flowers rather than sprinkling them evenly throughout a bouquet. Clustering allows single flower types to be fully examined and their colors to make a bolder statement. This dinner-party dessert station features a hand-blown Venetian-style vase filled with clivia, poppy, ranunculus, peach parrot tulip, golden 'Crème Upstar' tulip, maple flower, and clematis foliage.

Begin by placing the maple branches in an inverted triad, using firmer stems as braces for the flimsier ones. Three or four should suffice. Next, position clusters of like flowers. Depending on their stage of growth, some tulips will be stiffer than others. Let the floppy ones rest over the container's edge and use the firmer ones for the tallest part of the arrangement. Relax into the process and don't try to push a flower in a way that it doesn't want to go. One cluster of about five stems of coral clivia makes a beautiful burst on one side of the arrangement, while firm-stemmed ranunculuses are next, and finally twining vines.

Spontaneous side arrangements such as this clivia-filled etched cocktail glass are happy accidents, the result of fallen or inadvertently cut blossoms and an inspired container choice. Keep pretty glasses and jars near your worktable, and no flower will ever go wasted.

evening

clematis vines

MONTANA RUBENS
CLEMATIS

SPIREA

ANEMONE

WHITE RANUNCULUS

GREEN VIBURNUM

After spending the cool months inside all winter, the thought of going outdoors for dinner or a reception seems almost too good to be true. As soon as the days get longer, even if there's still a chill out, it feels great to put on an extra sweater and dine in the fresh air of spring.

A rustic, white cast-iron urn filled with white 'Montana Rubens' clematis, fluffy white spirea, white anemone, white ranunculus, and pale green viburnum makes a pristine centerpiece for this buffet on the porch. Urns are one of my favorite containers to work with because they raise the flowers up on pedestals, creating an elegant, old-fashioned effect. Their shape lends itself well to a triangular, three-dimensional formation. If you are fortunate enough to find them with handles, they are all the better for entwining vines. Nurseries, garden centers, and flea markets are the most likely places to find urns; often they're made of painted terra-cotta, which makes them less expensive and much easier to transport than those of cast iron.

Smaller arrangements flanking the urn are assembled in cast-off sections from an old ornate lamp. If you discover an odd cylinder or canister-shaped item, you can easily make it into a vase by inserting a water glass. These glasses are wrapped in organza sealed with a hot-glue gun to continue the white theme of the table.

To make an inner framework for the ranunculuses and anemones, crisscross the firm branches inside the urn, rotating it as you position the stems. This helps you to keep sight of the entire composition, avoiding two-dimensionality. (For obvious reasons, most table arrangements can't really afford to have a "front" and a "back.") Soon you'll have a crosshatch that will easily support the shorter, flimsier stems. To avoid a stiff look, which can easily happen with a stately container like this, let blossoms arch and droop over the edge. At first this may seem to make the shape lopsided and you might be tempted to "even things up," but in fact, a slight unevenness just makes each angle of the bouquet unique, so that the viewer wants to walk around it to appreciate each facet of the arrangement.

$spring$ *glossary*

ANEMONE

***ANEMONE;* RANUNCULACEAE**

Jewel-toned anemones open up like bright faces and are at their best in February and March. They come in scarlet, magenta, purple, crimson, lavender, and white, with some striped variations. White blossoms with black centers make a striking companion for spring's plum-edged ranunculus.

BERRIES

Dark blue, black, and red varieties contrast well with flower colors and can be used as an alternative to other kinds of foliage. Some favorites are hypericum, viburnum, and privet, all of which create texture.

BLUEBELL

***SCILLA;* LILIACEAE**

The deep violet blue and turquoise varieties of this springtime favorite add bold splashes of color.

BRANCHES

Lilac, cherry, quince, apple blossom, forsythia, magnolia, and dogwood are all great choices for simple, large arrangements. They work well in metal urns, galvanized buckets, or any container with an inverted triangle shape that is heavy enough to hold the weight of the branches.

CLEMATIS

***CLEMATIS;* RANUNCULACEAE**

There are over 200 species of clematis, but a favorite for arrangements is *C. armandii*. These scented white or soft pink flowers ('Hendersoni Rubra') have slender, dark green, pointed leaves. Once a rare sight in florist shops, they are being ordered from growers more and more. If you live in California, try planting some because the climate is kind to this variety. Its delicate, feminine tendrils are lovely in arrangements where long sprays can be draped, resembling tiny summer garden roses. The foliage is a good choice for both formal and rustic arrangements.

EUPHORBIA

***EUPHORBIA;* EUPHORBIACEAE**

Commonly called spurge, these flowers are actually masses of chartreuse or lime green bracts that make excellent filler, in the manner of Queen Anne's lace. They pair nicely with pink flowers, such as the green-centered pink ranunculus.

FORGET-ME-NOT

***MYOSOTIS;* BORAGINACEAE**

I think these flowers stand best by themselves, but with their yellow throats, they also look good with most small, yellow spring narcissus, ranunculuses, and buttercups, as well as delicate white flowers like paperwhites and lilies of the valley. Often seen in gardens as ground cover, the symbolism of these tiny but profuse, light blue blooms as an emblem of friendship makes them a traditional addition to bridal bouquets and nosegays.

FRITTILARY

***FRITTILARIA;* LILIACEAE**

A favorite species is the checkered, bell-shaped, plum-and-white *F. meleagris,* commonly called checkered or snake's-head lily, which also comes in a white-on-white form. It is usually quite short, so it lends itself to small, gemlike arrangements for shelves or windowsills. A taller variety, *F. persica,* has dusty sage green leaves and plum-brown petals. Another tall one is *F. imperialis,* which has a slightly skunky smell, so be sure to place it in a well-ventilated area.

GRAPE HYACINTH

***MUSCARI;* LILIACEAE**

The spring-flowering bulbs of the genus *Muscari,* with their upright stems and fleshy leaves, are prettiest when they stand alone. Their colors range from white to blue to dark purple. Simple, small glass containers are best for these Easter favorites. The supple thin stems can be braided easily for garlands or crowns.

HELLEBORE

***HELLEBORUS;* RANUNCULACEAE**

Available in many distinctive varieties. One gorgeous type is the *H. orientalis,* or Lenten rose, most common in early spring. It ranges in color from white to pink, red, maroon, purple, green, and yellow. Clusters of buds on drooping stems make exquisite bouquet additions; the paler versions are just right for a pristine effect. Another type, *H. foetidus,* is unusual, with clusters of celadon green bells, and adds a sense of drama to the featured wedding bouquet (page 57).

JASMINE

***JASMINUM;* OLEACEAE**

Because it's one of the sweetest-smelling flowers, just a few sprigs of *J. officinale grandiflorum* in a glass will add fragrance to any room. When planting, consult a garden book for species, as many are actually scentless. *J. nitidum, J. humile,* and *J. sambac* are all aromatic choices. Like most vines, jasmine adds a romantic touch to wedding bouquets, nosegays, and other feminine arrangements. It has a sensuous way of drooping and curving. Angelwing jasmine *(J. nitidum)* has spiky pink buds that add unusual texture to bouquets.

LILY OF THE VALLEY

***CONVALLARIA MAJALIS;* LILIACEAE**

Lily of the valley, the quintessential bridal flower, is said to symbolize purity and virginity. These drooping, bell-shaped, waxy white flowers have an intoxicating fragrance. They look very fetching by themselves or with other small white flowers.

NARCISSUS

***NARCISSUS;* AMARYLLIDACEAE**

This genus includes the popular spring daffodil and jonquil, as well as the paperwhite narcissus commonly force-bloomed indoors throughout winter. Most members of this group can stand to be out of water for several hours and so can be used alongside place settings on tables or tucked into vase handles.

PEONY

***PAEONIA;* PAEONIACEAE**

These fluffy, long-lasting blooms fall into two classes: herbaceous and tree peonies. I'm partial to the white-and-red-flecked 'Festiva Maxima', the soft pink 'Sarah Bernhardt', and the extraordinary deep scarlet 'Red Charm' varieties for their feminine curves and old-fashioned roselike scents.

POPPY

***PAPAVER;* PAPAVERACEAE**

P. nudicaule, commonly known as the Iceland poppy, is the best species for flower arranging. These leggy, cup-shaped flowers are lovely when combined with other blooms but they have a gorgeous simplicity all by themselves. Colors range from yellow to orange, salmon, rose, pink, cream, and white.

RANUNCULUS

***RANUNCULUS;* RANUNCULACEAE**

A relative of the buttercup, this fluffy, peony-shaped flower comes in white and many stunning shades of yellow, orange, pink, red, and purple. Also known as turban ranunculus, Persian ranunculus, and spring's rose, it is an excellent choice for simple bouquets and formal arrangements alike.

SNOWDROP

***GALANTHUS;* AMARYLLIDACEAE**

These nodding, bell-shaped white flowers look good in smaller arrangements with other delicate white flowers like smaller varieties of narcissus. Tiny clusters are good for wedding bouquets and boutonnieres.

TULIP

***TULIPA;* LILIACEAE**

'Apricot Parrot' is a peach-and-orange springtime favorite with "broken," or striped, and curly petals. Magenta and lily-like, the 'Ballade' has a narrower head and exotic, spiky petals. 'Black Parrots' are deep purple and crimson, with extremely frilly edges. Double-flowered tulips are large and multipetaled. They are a common sight in Dutch masters' paintings, where they are sometimes mistaken for peonies or cabbage roses.

VIBURNUM

***VIBURNUM;* CAPRIFOLIACEAE**

Prized for its foliage, flowers, fragrance, and berries, viburnum comes in colors ranging from white to yellow, pink, and acid green. Some of the showiest species are Japanese snowball *(V. plicatum),* doublefile viburnum *(V. tomentosum),* and laurustinus *(V. tinus).*

VIOLET

***VIOLA;* VIOLACEAE**

These tiny blossoms, along with their pansy cousins, look precious in almost any small container. A handful placed loosely in a teacup, shot glass, or silver saltcellar is ideal for a side table or powder room arrangement. The most famous variety is *V. odorata,* or sweet violet.

summertime
abundance

Summer begins subtly. One warm morning in late May, the faintest lavender scent floats alongside as you take a walk. As the days lengthen, you detect wisps of jasmine on the air at twilight. Sweet peas and sunflowers sneak into stalls at the farmers' market, showing off their colors. Sunlight lingers over lawns, and the phenomenon of warm grass wakes the senses to changes afoot. But these shy hints are only glimpses of the dazzle to come. Before you know it, you're presented with an astonishing array of flowers and fruits and the opportunities to celebrate them. Summer is the season of fat garden roses; country weddings; piles of peaches, plums, and tomatoes; lazy brunches that last until the afternoon; bare legs and shoulders; spontaneous picnics; long days; late suppers; and midnight swims.

Inspiration is everywhere you look at this time of year. Early morning excursions to garage sales and flea markets lead to all sorts of charming containers and table linens. Trips to markets and fruit stands in early summer remind me that cherry branches and spray roses complement each other perfectly, so I resolve to put more fruits and vegetables in my arrangements. Weekend getaways to the beach or the country are opportunities to record the natural world in a notebook or journal, jot down flower and color combinations, and collect snippets of uncommon plants and branches for planting at home.

This chapter revels in all the gifts of summer as it invites you to a garden wedding in Northern California's wine country, an iridescent birthday party where fruits are as much a part of the arrangements as flowers, and a brilliant feast that features summer's most triumphant vegetable (though it's technically a fruit!), the tomato, in several glorious courses. Even simple nasturtium flowers can create a lavish mood when the slanted light of a July day shines through their silky petals. Gorgeous roses, with poetic names like 'Perfume Delight', 'Wild at Heart', and 'The Alchemist', are stunning no matter where you place them, whether in Mason jars or polished silver urns. Other inspired containers include wire baskets, silver sugar bowls, and vintage ceramic vases.

Casual, almost careless beauty is the goal with these projects, never fussiness. But there is much to be said, as famed gardener and hostess Vita Sackville-West once put it, for "sweet disorder . . . judiciously arranged." Words to live by, in art and life, in summer or all year-round.

iridescent
birthday party

Inspiration comes from many sources. A shimmering, Florentine-glass cake plate compelled me to consider iridescence and its magical qualities. It is present so often in summer: in the sunlit moisture on garden leaves, on the shimmery surfaces of plums and blueberries, on the wings of lazy dragon-flies and june bugs, in the glow of candlelight on a gossamer party dress.

Iridescence has an appealing, now-you-see-it, now-you-don't quality, like the ephemeral nature of summer itself, and thus seemed appropriate for a birthday celebration. Using the cake plate as a centerpiece, I began improvising to create this arrangement. Hunting around at a flea market for blue-green accents, I tried to echo the colors of the plate with a few teal and turquoise ceramic vases. These milky, opalescent serving dishes and harlequin tumblers had exactly the right summery gleam. Bringing together all of these elements, I created a setting that would promi-nently feature the fairy-tale cake on its platter. Festooned with wrapped candies, glittery party hats, and place cards, the table doubles as a place to set favors and gifts.

Garden roses, like the plush 'Evelyn' shown here, are the floral stars at this time of year, but it would be a shame not to include some of

summer's gorgeous fruits in your work, as they sometimes rival the flowers themselves in their sensuous beauty. Blueberries and viburnum are used here, but you might forage for other, similarly textured branches in your neighborhood.

Early summer is the best time for using fruit branches, as the fruit is small, firm, and securely attached to the branch. Start by placing the blueberry and plum branches, which act as a kind of framework. Even in smaller arrangements, it's helpful to have a bit of structure around which to position the rest of the blossoms. Next, work in the privet berries and then the garden roses. There are many pale pink, yellow, and white varieties that would contrast just as well. The key

element is a luxuriant, full-blown rose. Fat roses add a sense of summery lushness to these vertical vases and leggy branches. This particular rose is very frilly, almost a flower within a flower, and is extremely aromatic.

After placing the biggest flowers, add smaller blooms like the white hydrangea sprigs here, which help to fill out the bouquet. A quick way to position an additional plum or apricot exactly where you want it is to take a small, unattached piece of fruit and simply pierce it with a spare branch. If you push it deep within the arrangement, it will fill the space and no one will ever guess you cheated a little.

In the larger vase, I also added passion vine, a favorite finishing touch of mine. Its pliable stem can be looped out of the vase and back in by entwining it around a branch or even the handle of the pitcher, as I did here. I like to wind the vine down so it touches the table and then up above the flower tops so that its leaves are clearly visible. With its curlicues and tendrils, passion vine adds a lovely sort of wildness, making your bouquet look natural, like something you'd find in a hidden lane or an overgrown garden. (Other vines with the same flexibility include sweet pea, star jasmine, akebia, and potato vine.) Finally, scatter a few fallen plums and apricots about the table and you'll really feel like you've conjured a summertime orchard indoors.

summer wedding *in the country*

Summer weddings are as popular as ever, featuring some of the season's most exquisite blossoms: garden roses, hydrangeas, dahlias, sweet peas, and clematis. If you have your heart set on a certain kind of flower for a wedding, make sure that you set the date during that flower's season. While many varieties can be flown in year-round, you'll get the very best selection if you keep the season in mind. Many a June bride has had to make do with small, sad tulips when she could have had sensational, frilly parrot tulips if only she'd tied the knot in March. If you've chosen a time of year not suited to the garden roses you love, open your mind to a florist's alternatives. Generally, they know what's most available and lovely at any given time.

If you don't have a specific favorite, think about colors you like, personality traits you'd like to express, or a style you hope the wedding itself will convey. Most brides have a certain kind of dress in mind; if you've chosen a gown that is romantic, classic, old-fashioned, vintage, or contemporary, that too can help clarify flower choices. I have the same philosophy for wedding bouquets and arrangements as I do in all my other work: I want the individual flowers to stand out, in as natural a style as possible. Delicate colors and bud forms can be lost when blooms are too tightly packed or forced into artificial

shapes. Have faith that if you pick the freshest flowers for your event, they will naturally do for you what they do best: exist in radiance.

This garden full of summer roses is a dreamlike setting for a wedding. The bride's bouquet and table arrangements are simple and natural, in keeping with her style and the flowers in the garden. Her choices of

summertime blooms are some of my favorites as well: peonies, 'Graham Thomas' garden roses, clematis, hellebores, mock orange, five-leaf akebia, and ash pods.

To make the bouquet, begin by clustering two roses with a peony. Then create another grouping of green hellebores, white clematis, and ash pods. A third cluster consists of another rose, a peony, and a ranunculus. When you pull the three groups together with a rubber band, there's a natural-looking asymmetrical quality to the bouquet. This method of grouping like with like often makes even the most common flowers combine in an exotic way. Finally, fill in loose areas with the mock orange and akebia vine. Be sure to position the flowers loosely, so that they are touching but are not too close together.

The finishing touch on the bride's bouquet is, of course, the ribbon or fabric. I made several loose loops with about two yards of dyed pink silk ribbon, stapled the loops at the center, wired the "bow" to the bouquet, then trimmed each end with a V-shaped cutout, called a swallow's tail cut. I prefer loops or even straight ribbon to a traditional bow, which can often appear fussy. An alternative to ribbon is light fabric cut or folded about three to five inches wide. Loop the material so that it drapes over the bride's hand. Try it several ways and see which one most reflects her own style.

The bride's bouquet is echoed here in the table arrangements, which are essentially made up of the same flowers. The most important aspect of these bouquets, I think, is that they not obscure the guests' views of one another across the table. For receptions, I almost always choose low containers and I cut the stems very short, allowing the blooms to tumble over the vase edge. The informality of this particular party, with its fluffy rose hedges and French café chairs, led me to use a hammered-silver teapot and its companion sugar bowl and creamer for the bride's and groom's table. I found mismatched antique silver pitchers and pots for the other guests. If the prospect of gathering several unusual containers is daunting, remember that many caterers or florists will loan them for a fee.

nasturtium

picnic table

ORANGE, RED, AND
YELLOW NASTURTIUMS
ON TRAILING VINES

ALPINE STRAWBERRY
BRANCHES

In certain parts of the country, the climbing, trailing vines of fiery nasturtiums cover banks, fences, rocks, and tree stumps all summer long. On an August drive through the wine country of Northern California, it's not uncommon to see perky nasturtiums and their round emerald leaves blanketing the roadside for miles. When making arrangements for outdoor settings, I try as much as possible to draw inspiration from the environment itself. If I'm shopping for a picnic with friends, I know I can pick up a bunch of cosmos or daisies to decorate with, but it feels much more authentic (and challenging!) to utilize some of the natural materials at hand. When you decide to use whatever you can find, it forces you to be creative.

For this late outdoor luncheon, the guests gathered a few armfuls of the profuse nasturtiums growing under this wisteria arbor, and we combined them with another summertime favorite, alpine strawberry vines. When cutting the nasturtiums, retain as much stem and leaf as possible to help anchor the flimsy vines. Choose a wide-mouthed vase so that there's plenty of room to let the tendrils and blossoms spread out.

To make this arrangement, first position the strawberries, then work in the nasturtiums. Push the ends deep into the vase and let the vines trail over the lip, all the way to the table surface if you like. Fill in blank areas with shorter stems. Consider garnishing the plates with a few blossoms (the nasturtium flower is edible). When you're working with a single flower variety, as long as you don't pack the blossoms too densely, it's almost impossible to overdo it—so feel free to let yourself go wild! Other edible herbs that make clever nosegays for a breakfast or brunch table include rosemary, mint, chives, basil, sage, fennel, and oregano.

tuberose and citrus *illumination*

Sultry nights inspire all kinds of spontaneous get-togethers, like this intimate cocktail party in a tiny city garden. The simplicity of white in an evening setting works beautifully, especially when the background has lots of dark foliage. Against all the deep green leaves, darker colors tend to recede while these creamy tuberoses glow. The oranges also have a lovely luminescent quality, especially in delicate candlelight.

Sweet-smelling flowers like tuberose and jasmine tend to become even more fragrant at nighttime, adding a touch of romance and striking an ideal mood for an evening party. To begin this arrangement, position the orange branches, using them as a framework for the tuberoses. The more the branches crisscross inside the urn, the easier it will be to secure the other flowers. When working with branches, it's important to allow as much water as possible to penetrate the woody stems, hydrating fruits and leaves. Use clippers to cut an X shape at the end of each stem. Next, add the tuberoses. They have fairly flexible stems, so you might try curving them here and there. I always cut the stems one at a time, varying lengths as necessary. Because the bouquet is three-dimensional, try to rotate the vase as you work, making small adjustments with each new addition. Allow the flowers to tumble over the edge of the container, to give the whole piece a relaxed and natural appearance.

It's fun to experiment with candles. We used pillars as well as votives in glass holders to warm up the setting, but tapers in understated candelabras would also work. Use unscented varieties so that the delicate perfume of the flowers isn't overpowered. You can make cleaning the glass holders easier if you remember to put a tablespoon of water in each before placing candles inside. The day after the party, the remaining wax can be easily removed with a butter knife. Rinse containers in warm water and wipe off residue with a dish towel. Tiny tea lights in metal canisters can also be used inside votive holders, though they don't burn as long as the freestanding type.

Conversation areas at cocktail parties are the perfect places for extremely aromatic flowers such as the tuberose, gardenia, and lily. These would be overpowering in a dinner setting but are welcome, sensuous fragrances in open areas where guests mingle. Smaller bouquets—like the ones here made of tuberoses, star-of-Bethlehem, calla lilies, and ornamental green oranges—can be strategically placed for unexpected bursts of scent.

tomato f e a s t

Although roses, berries, and juicy plums and peaches are emblematic of summer's riches, no trip to a farmers' market at this time of year would be complete without a few pounds of voluptuous, ripe tomatoes. I start out leisurely, wandering among the stalls before breakfast, comparing varieties and colors and flavors, then sampling morsels wherever they're offered. Finally, when I've surveyed all of the plump golden, orange, green, red, and pink globes, I grab a wooden flat and begin piling it up with my favorites.

Due to the diligence and passion of organic farmers, more and more people are rediscovering the taste and texture of real tomatoes, the kind your grandmother used to talk about, which are nothing like the flavorless lumps grocery store chains have promoted for years. We're now seeing varieties that are not only tangy and delicious but also stunning to look at. Heirloom strains like 'Purple Marvel', 'Brandywine', 'Zebra-Stripe', 'Watermelon', and 'Sungold' result not only in delectable suppers but also in marvelous arrangements. Inspired by the sheer profusion of these beauties, some cooks have begun a

summertime tradition of creating a meal where each course is made with tomatoes, from breads and appetizers to the main course and right on through to dessert. Decorating the tables for this feast is fun but, of course, devouring all the delicious dishes is even better.

For a tomato-based arrangement, use the most exotic-looking tomatoes you can find and make sure to get lots of different sizes. Stems of cherry tomatoes and others on the vine add natural greenery. If you're limited to one or two types, get a quantity of these and add other bright vegetable elements. Ornamental peppers are fairly common and can add orange, green, and yellow accents. If you add a floral element, choose one that won't outshine the main ingredient. I chose petite 'Maitland' spray roses with their delicate buds intact. The urn and French garden vases are rustic accompaniments to the picnic table.

summer *glossary*

AKEBIA

***AKEBIA QUINATA;* LARDIZABALACEAE**

My favorite species of this deciduous vine is the chocolate-purple *quinata,* commonly called five-leaf akebia. Its delicate foliage and supple stems are ideal for entwining and cascading, as in the wedding table arrangements (pages 54–57).

BEGONIA

***BEGONIA;* BEGONIACEAE**

Lacy white, pink, orange, or red clusters with succulent petals, these are easy plants to grow in containers and cut from year-round. They're short, so they work best in petite arrangements.

COREOPSIS

***COREOPSIS;* COMPOSITAE**

A Mason jar filled with a profusion of these yellow, orange, maroon, or reddish daisies looks like a whirl of summer butterflies.

COSMOS

***COSMOS;* COMPOSITAE**

The daisylike flowers of *C. bipinnatus* come in pink, rose, lavender, purple, or crimson, with puffy yellow centers. I use chocolate cosmos (*C. astrosanguineus*) in both late summer and early fall arrangements.

DELPHINIUM

***DELPHINIUM;* RANUNCULACEAE**

These spires look lovely just by themselves in very tall vases. They're well known for a deep blue variety but can also be found in white, light blue, and shades of red, pink, lavender, purple, and yellow. Delphiniums work well for large rooms with high ceilings as they can be up to four feet tall.

FRUIT BRANCHES

Essential to many summertime arrangements, branches provide structure while their fruits convey the abundance of the season. They should be incorporated naturally, without wires, and as early in the summer as possible to prevent the ripe fruits from detaching. I use peach, plum, blueberry, and green almond branches. Alpine strawberries and raspberries sometimes grow on vinelike stems and can also add spots of color.

FUCHSIA

***FUCHSIA;* ONAGRACEAE**

For an arrangement where you want a hot, tropical effect, hybrid fuchsias, with their magenta and purple color bursts, are perfect. The sepals (the top parts that flare back) are almost always white, red, or pink. The inside part of the flower (corolla) can be red, pink, blue violet, purple, white, or sometimes orange. Fuchsias complement acid green nicotiana, roses, dahlias, and other hot-colored summer flowers.

GARDENIA

***GARDENIA;* RUBIACEAE**

Glossy bright green leaves and highly aromatic white blossoms are the trademarks of this classically romantic flower. Varieties include 'August Beauty', 'Golden Magic', and 'Mystery'.

HYDRANGEA

***HYDRANGEA;* SAXIFRAGACEAE**

Old-fashioned and showy, these clusters of long-lasting flowers come in white, pink, red, green, lavender, and blue.

MARIGOLD

***CALENDULA OFFICINALIS;*
COMPOSITAE**

Marigolds are wild-seeming orange or yellow short flowers. They tend to look best by themselves in simple, dark containers that contrast well with their bright petals.

MOCK ORANGE

PHILADELPHUS; **SAXIFRAGACEAE**

These fragrant white blooms smell faintly of citrus. They bring a frilly softness to small bouquets and are prized for their arching boughs in larger arrangements.

NASTURTIUM

TROPAEOLUM; **TROPAEOLUM**

These peppery, edible blossoms are often used in salads and they make excellent, long-lasting cut flowers. Their bold, bright colors such as gold, orange, and scarlet are emblematic of summer, and the flowers lend themselves well to simple, free-flowing arrangements. While nasturtiums are rarely sold in flower markets, they grow easily and in profusion. Plant some seedlings in May, and you'll have masses of silky blossoms come summer.

NICOTIANA

NICOTIANA; **SOLANACEAE**

A relative of tobacco, this tubular, fragrant flower opens up like a five-pointed star and comes in white, pink, red, and (my personal favorite) lime green. When I want to make a bouquet look as though I have just picked it from my yard, I use nicotiana.

PASSION VINE

PASSIFLORA; **PASSIFLORACEAE**

This flower is said to symbolize the passion of Christ (hence the name), with a lacy corona that resembles a halo or crown of thorns. It is aromatic and wraps easily, with tendrils that you can attach to containers and other flowers for unusual effects. In bell and star shapes, the flower comes in solid white, purple, mixed purple and white, coral, yellow, and dark red.

ROSE

ROSA; **ROSACEAE**

From single to double to cabbage to heirloom to hybrid teas, glorious summer garden roses include 'Golden Celebration', the perfumed pink 'Evelyn', 'Mr. Lincoln', with its deep magenta petals, 'Brandy', 'Othello', 'Tropicana', 'Tequila Sunrise', and many, many more. Unlike the sturdy, erect hothouse varieties seen from December to April, these are primarily grown outdoors from late spring until fall, and each blossom seems to have a distinct personality. Stems are more likely to be flexible, fragrances are much more pronounced, and their overall effect is more graceful and natural. Whenever possible, choose a garden rose over all others!

TUBEROSE

POLIANTHES TUBEROSA; **AGAVACEAE**

Powerful, heady perfume and creamy white blossoms characterize this elegant, waxy flower. Its fragrance becomes even stronger at night, especially on warm summer evenings.

VIBURNUM

VIBURNUM; **CAPRIFOLIACEAE**

These branches are available in a range of sizes and have berries in colors from yellow, red, and orange to vibrant blues, such as the *V. davidii,* shown in our iridescent birthday party arrangement (page 50). Berries are useful for adding texture and unusual color bursts.

ZINNIA

ZINNIA; **COMPOSITAE**

These bright, round-headed garden favorites come in many fiery colors, like mahogany red, yellow, and orange, but my favorite is the *Z. elegans* variety called 'Green Envy' because its intense chartreuse sets off the brighter shades of summer bouquets. Zinnias look great all by themselves; crowded into a mason jar or ceramic crock, they are simple and old-fashioned.

fall *colors*

When the poet Stephen Yenser wrote "the fire in all things loves the end of them," he was describing the last hurrahs of autumn. Even if you don't live where the landscape burns brightly at summer's end, you probably notice the alchemy of the seasons in other ways. Change is literally in the air in September and October, as soft morning dew gives way to mist and frost. The quality of sunlight changes as the days shorten, and late afternoons seem washed in red-gold liquid, like the season's cider. The smell of wood-burning stoves drifts through twilight air, and the plump moon hangs heavy, deep yellow. Roman mythology marks harvesttime as the transition of power from Flora, the goddess of spring and summer flowers, to Pomona and Ceres, goddesses of fruitfulness and agriculture.

After the pastels and pinks and pale greens of spring flowers and the hot colors of summer blossoms, I welcome the warmer, deeper colors that appear in fall. Dahlias, with their gold, brown, and plum faces, beckon. Sunflowers grow tall along roadsides. Fall fruits and vegetables are like orange, red, yellow, and purple baubles. Quinces, pumpkins, persimmons, grapes, pomegranates, rose hips, acorn squash, olives, and crab apples all find their way into my shopping cart and table arrangements at this time of year. Afternoon walks in the woods often produce armfuls of burnished leaves that make glowing bouquets and garlands.

As the days become cooler, it feels satisfying to create warm, inviting settings using all the rich elements the season offers. This chapter explores several different ways of bringing the outdoors in, inspired by fall's vibrant turning. Golden afternoon light in a sitting room showcases deep plum dahlias surrounded by persimmon leaves and fruit. A bright juxtaposition of peppers, eggplants, and orange callas turns a kitchen table into a treasure trove of farmers' market bounty. Cascading olive branches and chinaberries blaze in amber sunlight along with a handful of red peonies,

providing a welcome variation on traditional autumn colors, while red roses and dusky grapes overflow from a Thanksgiving compote, offering a new twist on the idea of a harvest cornucopia. Even a stark, contemporary dining room benefits from fall's lavish gifts when we create a dahlia-and-cosmo-filled centerpiece as a stylistic counterbalance.

Most of us spent so many Septembers as children returning to school, to structure and new learning experiences; perhaps that's why autumn seems to epitomize change. Welcome it by taking time to notice the slowness and grace with which this season comes upon us and how it begins to dissolve the past, making way for future beauty. Even in warm climates, if we are very observant, we can witness this transition and learn from it.

plum dahlias
and persimmons

As late summer gives way to fall, garden roses appear less often at my favorite farmers' market and are soon replaced by an equally resplendent bloomer, the dahlia. Like the mania inspired by tulips in the 1600s, a dahlia craze in the 1800s brought forth rabid cultivation of hybrids and strains, resulting in hundreds of varieties and shades. In autumn I gravitate toward the boldest colors—the deep garnets, purples, oranges, and browns. These stiff-stemmed pompons are stunning all by themselves but look even prettier when combined with fruit branches of the season. Dahlias don't bloom much after they're cut, so it's best to pick them when they're mature, though smaller offshoots may eventually open a bit. Not naturally long-lasting, they'll remain upright and fresh looking for three to four days in water.

Plum-colored 'Thomas Edison' dahlias stand out against orange arbutus baubles, persimmon branches, and orange persimmon foliage in a wide-mouthed ceramic pitcher. Other vases, containing only dahlias, brighten up the mantel and window areas. In the large bouquet, the foliage is as important as the flowers themselves. While I often see persimmon branches, stems with leaves intact are somewhat rare. Even a handful by itself makes a pretty autumn bouquet. Their orange, yellow, and green striations are breathtaking when sunlight glows through them. The color of the leaves resonates with the orange

arbutus, which adds a knobby, textured effect. This particular dahlia features very velvety petals, which contrast nicely with the shiny elements of the arrangement. As you forage and shop for flowers, treat yourself to the tactile pleasures of experimenting with texture.

If you're using weighty blossoms and branches with fruit, make sure you have a heavy container to keep the arrangement from toppling. This saffron-colored ceramic pitcher is a sturdy choice. Begin by placing three persimmon branches, crossing them inside the vase to maintain balance. Position the dahlias next and finish off with sprigs of leaves.

When you're lucky enough to find plump, colorful fruits in fall, don't hide them in the kitchen. Instead, group persimmons, pomegranates, or miniature pumpkins around your arrangements and offerings like little sculptures.

farmers' market *harvest*

In the fall, I find myself at the local farmers' market for hours, choosing unusual gourds, roots, tubers, beans, and other vegetables to mix with autumn flowers. I love walking into my kitchen toting full canvas sacks and tumbling this bright bounty onto my table. Rather than seeking out specific varieties, I try to keep an open mind so that color itself becomes the inspiration. This encourages me to try out combinations I might not have experimented with before, like complementary orange with blue.

Rusty gold and orange callas and marigolds suited this turquoise McCoy pottery, while yellow and orange peppers paired well with deep purple Italian and Asian eggplants in a matching blue bowl. Many vegetables, like peppers, tomatoes, and squash, don't need to be refrigerated. Why hide them when you can have so much fun incorporating their shades and shapes into assemblages anywhere in the house, even on a coffee table as shown here. These flame-colored lilies look dyed but they are in fact hybridized and grown naturally. Aside from traditional white, other shades include pink, red, burgundy, and even black.

Callas have a wonderful Art Deco quality, but can be very stiff-looking. For a more rustic setting where you want a looser effect, choose

a wide-mouthed container or one with a ruffled edge like the vase shown here. Cut stems to varying lengths for an even fuller appearance.

A word about using foliage with this flower: They really look best by themselves. With their sculptured, clean lines, hardly any greenery does them justice. If anything, they work best with their own leaves. While they are big drinkers, fresh callas can easily last the length of a dinner party out of water, hand tied and laid alongside place settings. Recut and hydrate them in vases when your event is over.

olive branches
and peonies

RED CHARM PEONIES
OLIVE BRANCHES
ELAEAGNUS LEAVES
CHINABERRY BRANCHES

Although peonies are not necessarily fall flowers, when I come upon a rare handful at this time of year, I can't resist seeing their rich colors and full forms paired with the leggy olive and chinaberry branches that become available during these months. Nestled up against the flower heads themselves are acid green chinaberries and dark green elaeagnus leaves, which contrast with and frame the blood red blossoms. These fiery bold reds and golds, offset by silvery green, are exquisitely evocative of autumn and a welcome alternative to the shades of orange we often associate with the season.

Prized for their rich history as symbols of peace, olive branches have a splendid cascading quality and prettily shaped leaves. Black, green, or nearly purple, the shiny olives provide contrast to their matte foliage; scattering them alongside a table-top arrangement conjures a harvest motif. When preparing olive branches, make sure to strip foliage near the olives themselves to showcase the fruit.

Chinaberries are long-lasting, bright globes that reaffirm the idea of a harvest offering while adding excellent shape, contrast, and texture. After forming the basic shape of the arrangement by placing the olive branches and peonies, add the chinaberries last, generously grouping them to create bursts of color.

There are certain flowers that capture one's attention and refuse to let go. Walk into a room where even a single peony reposes in a simple glass, and it's almost impossible not to become mesmerized by the sheer mass of its crenellated petals and saturated, opaque shades. New Zealand–grown types like the 'Red Charm' shown here are still available through early fall. Sometimes called the "twenty-day flower," peonies last an extremely long time. It's best to buy them when they're just beginning to unfold; these buds took about three days to open fully. Peonies are especially prized in Japan and China and are often seen in paintings and textiles, so they're an appropriate choice for the Asian-inspired decor of this sitting room.

café au lait *and chocolate*

SNOWBERRIES

CAFÉ AU LAIT DAHLIAS

JAPANESE ANEMONES

CHOCOLATE COSMOS

It's tempting to put a spare, vertical arrangement into a modern retro dining room like this, but the sleek lines here actually benefit from a looser, fuller bouquet that alleviates the starkness of the setting. A deep, old-fashioned amber glass compote filled with snowberry sprays, creamy pink-beige 'Café au Lait' dahlias, and chocolate cosmos is lush and welcoming while its lines remain simple. You actually have more freedom than you might think in this sort of room, as it presents an almost-blank canvas upon which to experiment. To take advantage of the room's stunning green walls, I chose shades of beige, pink, cream, and brown for contrast. An alternative to the mixed bouquet here might be to use masses of just a single variety, like 'Casablanca' lilies, callas, sunflowers or even interesting foliage like green or cocoa-colored smoke bush.

To make the arrangement, start with the snowberries, crisscrossing branches in the vase to brace first the dahlias and then the cosmos. Another way to express lavishness in an austere setting is to add smaller satellites like this brindled glass full of chocolate cosmos.

It's also fun to try your hand at oversized arrangements when you have the opportunity. When a room is more of a showplace than a dinner party setting, you have the freedom to use a larger container, such as an urn. As long as you keep the scale in mind, you can create "masterpieces" using taller stems.

days of grapes
and roses

Traditionally, a cornucopia symbolizes fall's bounty—one is often seen in painted still lifes and on Thanksgiving tables. This ceramic compote full of fall fruits and flowers is a variation on the theme. To make an assemblage like this, you are really just playing with the elements, positioning and repositioning the fruits and petals just as if you were making a collage with paper images, until you come up with a tableau that's pleasing to the eye. As with all flower arranging, give yourself plenty of time to relax into the activity. I find that arranging becomes almost meditative. Another enjoyable aspect of making assemblages is that you can change them from day to day, until the flowers fade (or the tempting fruit disappears!), by adding or removing elements, rotating the container, or rearranging nearby objects.

Other ingredients that may work well in a compote are miniature pumpkins, persimmons, figs, branches of plump rose hips, tiny sprays of baby pomegranates, or crab apples. You might also want to experiment with fabric or ribbon in an arrangement like this. Before adding the flowers, loosely drape wide satin ribbon over and through the fruits, letting the ends cascade onto the table surface. For additional embellishment, fabric can also be placed into the compote bowl before setting fruit inside. For a very long table, two or three fruit-and-flower-filled compotes look inviting when interspersed with lower vase arrangements.

To make the center-piece, place plump grapes and pears in tiers to keep the fruit from toppling. Once you've positioned the fruit, add a few rose clusters or loose petals. To make a cluster, first clip the rose head from its stem. Holding the petals tightly where they meet the flower base, gently pull the ball of petals away from the base and release it, upside down. Eventually, it will relax into a nest of petals. If you can manage to drape a few of the grapes still on their stems over the dish edge, the effect is even more painterly. Additional arrangements feature rust-colored 'Terra Cotta' roses, blue hydrangeas, euphorbia, and madrone, a kind of arbutus that tumbles nicely from tin plant holders.

An inexpensive way to add color to a table setting is to experiment with tapers. In this case, the sienna candles have a color-layering effect in keeping with the flowers, fruit, and lacquered artwork on the walls. A saffron candle against a lime tablecloth was such a fortuitous combination that it once inspired me to repaint a whole kitchen in those colors! Similarly, I've seen rooms utterly transformed with the addition of a single candle-stick placed near a full-blown rose in a juice glass.

fall *glossary*

CHINESE LANTERNS
ABUTILON; MALVACEAE
Also called flowering maple and Chinese bellflower, this shrub's flowers have a color and shape reminiscent of pumpkins, so they look good massed together, even when dried, for autumnal occasions. Chinese lantern holds well, and its many different flowers combine beautifully with spring, summer, and fall flowers. For a sexy bouquet, try combining 'Red Charm' peonies with Chinese lanterns, akebia, and purple miniature plum foliage.

COCKSCOMB
CELOSIA; AMARANTHACEAE
Cockscomb, whether fan shaped, like *C.* 'Cristata', or clustered and plumed, like *C* 'Plumosa', is a velvety, sculptured addition that comes in brilliant shades of yellow, orange, crimson, gold, red, and even lime green. Cockcomb does well in compact arrangements since its most interesting feature, resembling the undulations of a rooster's crest, is best seen from above. It makes a very unusual addition to an autumnal bridal bouquet.

COSMOS
COSMOS; COMPOSITAE
The bright yellow centers of *C. bipinnatus* are framed by rose, pink, magenta, lavender, brown, or white petals. One of my favorites, chocolate cosmos *(C. atrosanguineus)*, is available from early until late fall.

CRAB APPLE
MALUS; ROSACEAE
Crab apples come in many shapes and sizes, from quite large to as small as blueberries. Red, green, yellow, or golden orange, they are ideal additions to late summer and fall arrangements and work especially well with garden roses, dahlias, and sunflowers.

DAHLIA
DAHLIA; COMPOSITAE
'Thomas Edison', with its velvety purple heads, can be up to six inches in width and pairs well with deep blue-green hydrangea. It also makes a gorgeous statement alongside a dark purple garden rose called 'The Prince', and its color stands out in celadon-and-white arrangements. 'Café au Lait' is an exquisite beige or creamy peach. Dahlias come as small as silver dollars and as large as dinner plates. Their glory is brief, but for the few days they grace your table, they are stunning. Recut and refill vases often, as their stems can create murky water.

FALL FOLIAGE
Depending on where you live, you will likely have access to some sort of turning leaves as the temperature changes. Maple on the East Coast, while splendid, barely lasts a day. A hardier favorite is copper beech, with variegated white-edged purple leaves. All beech leaves have a graceful form for large and small arrangements. Burning bush *(Euonymous atropurpurea)* turns a fantastic bright pink on the East Coast. If you can get hold of persimmon foliage, take advantage of it for a day; its beauty is vivid though fleeting.

FRUIT BRANCHES

Some of the best texture providers are branches of quinces, pears, apples, crab apples, pomegranates, and persimmons. Arrangements with fruit suggest plenitude and grace. A bowl of quince fruit next to your bed is heavenly as you drift off to sleep.

ROSE HIPS

ROSA; ROSACEAE

These are the cup-shaped fruitlets of the rose plant that appear after the flowers have dropped off. Cutting a few canes with these red, pink, or pale orange bulbs not only adds a wild texture to arrangements but also helps the plant produce better blooms the following season.

SMOKE BUSH / SMOKE TREE

COTINUS COGGYGRIA; ANACARDIACEAE

Available in red, green, and plum, this adds a matte-velvet texture and works particularly well in large arrangements, as the branches are leggy. Try the dark plum with plum dahlias and 'Sweet Autumn' clematis. Serves as a perfect backdrop for rusty orange garden roses.

SNOWBERRY

SYMPHORICARPOS; CAPRIFOLIACEAE

S. albus is a shrub that produces plump white berries after its flowers fall off. These last well in arrangements, where they look like festive baubles. Also available in a pearly baby pink. Try the white version with elderberries, creamy 'Fair Bianca', garden roses, furry clematis seed heads, and lamb's ears for a velvety soft, very romantic arrangement.

SUNFLOWER

HELIANTHUS; COMPOSITAE

With their cheerful, big faces, sunflowers look wonderful in canisters all by themselves but they also make nice additions to shorter, rounder arrangements. The fluffy, double-headed yellow 'Teddy Bear' is a favorite, along with 'Autumn Beauty', whose petals can be reddish, rust, brown, or gold. I usually try to conceal nubbly stems within the container or behind other flowers. While cut sunflowers last up to seven days, their beautiful leaves tend to dry out earlier and should be trimmed as needed.

VIBURNUM

VIBURNUM; CAPRIFOLIACEAE

Orange, yellow, red, and several shades of blue characterize these shiny berry clusters. They add a pleasing shape and texture to many arrangements. V. davidii, V. opulus, and V. sargentii 'Onondaga' are all colorful choices.

a winter's tale

As T. S. Eliot wrote, "The end is where we start from." Nature provides time for all living things to rest, regenerate, and gather strength for a new cycle. Winter is a time for slowing down, looking inward, and contemplating the year that's passed. Cold weather encourages people to spend time indoors and to share hearty, comforting meals, while the holidays allow further opportunities to be at home with loved ones. The charms of winter include glittering night skies, chilly cheeks, the stark beauty of bare branches, cozy woolen clothing, and the exchanging of gifts.

If you live where the temperatures sink low, you might notice that subtleties become more apparent when the landscape is covered in white. In winter, it's a meditative act to quietly watch the way light hits snow, how the sky's color changes, how the colors of tree bark stand out against muted winter tones.

In the Berkshires where I grew up, winters last a long time, and in those months while the plants hibernate, even the slightest bit of color is a wonder to behold. Days end early, and one has to work a little harder to bring cheer into one's world. It has been said that long before Christianity took hold, pagans and others who celebrated the winter solstice brought evergreens and other plants indoors to provide aromatic symbols of hope and promise of the warmer seasons to come. My mother would often cut bare branches of forsythia and force them indoors, coaxing sunny yellow blossoms into our kitchen for weeks at a time. A trip to the nursery sent us home with African violets, geraniums, and cyclamen for dashes of crimson and violet.

You may want to create your own indoor cutting garden, where you can clip from blooming geranium, begonia, and fuchsia to make small, colorful arrangements anytime, even when there's snow on the ground. Even if you live in warmer climates, you'll find joy in watching a crop of frilly paperwhite narcissus or dramatic red amaryllis evolve from bulbs as you busy yourself with preparations for wintertime get-togethers. To get you into the spirit of foraging for the beauty this season has to offer, here are several wintertime arrangements, some elegant, some romantic, some created simply to cheer up a room that looks out over a chilly landscape. Our cocktail party with glowing candles and hot-colored poppies is so sizzling it could ward off an ice storm. Even though it's cold outside, you will have a great time improvising a centerpiece with indoor succulents, brightening up corners of your house with pitchers of hyacinths, creating an orchid-filled dinner party, or making an intimate rose-petal-strewn table for two on Valentine's night.

It's easy to appreciate the flower arts when everything's in bloom; the challenge at this time of year is to maintain your passion for living things throughout the long months of scarcity. And consider this while you're longing for the cold and damp to end, dreaming of peonies, lilacs, and tulips: all of these gorgeous flowers require a few months of frost in order to blossom next spring.

hot *poppies*

YELLOW, ORANGE,
ROSE, PINK, AND CREAM
ICELANDIC POPPIES

STAR 2000 ROSES

A friend's intriguing idea of hot colors on a cold night led to this winter-time cocktail party. The hostess imagined shiny fabrics, sequins, rustling skirts, cocktails in exotic glasses, and couples scattered about, engaged in whispered conversations. Keeping those visions in mind, we decided to showcase the hot pinks, yellows, and oranges of a winter favorite, the Icelandic poppy. With dozens of glowing votive candles wrapped in silk and bright poppies illuminated by candles, we transformed the whole room into a sensual, intimate setting.

Poppies are sexy, with their ruffly skirts, bright colors, unusual fragrance, and fuzzy buds. They're easy to arrange by simply cutting them at varying lengths. For these bouquets we used about a dozen stems per glass, making sure to include a few buds in each. Poppies are also fairly inexpensive, especially when you consider how showy they are. The glass cylinders here are some of the cheapest containers you can find. All you need to transform them is a glue gun and some pretty fabric, like this raw silk in hot pink and gold. You can use the same technique with votive candle-holders: Wrap the containers with a few inches of fabric and secure the ends with a seam of hot glue. When making the cylinders, it helps to lay them horizontally on your work surface, set one edge of material with glue, then roll the glass until the other edge matches up. *Voilà!* The vases are so appealing (and inexpensive), you can give them away as party favors when the evening's over—filled with flowers, of course!

Another theatrical feature of this table is the use of rose petals. For parties, weddings, or any festive occasion where guests will be table-hopping, you can create natural confetti with petals. An unusual way to present them is to make pulled rose clusters, displaying the inner structure of the

rose. Here, we used a stunning lipstick-colored variety called 'Star 2000'. To begin, clip the rose head from its stem. Holding the petals tightly where they meet the flower base, gently pull the ball of petals away from the base and release it, upside down, on the table. Pale edges will be visible, and eventually the petals will relax into a natural sculpture, or nest, of petals, loosening and scattering as the night wears on. Like the candles, these should be numerous and placed at will.

Transforming an environment for night is much easier than one might think. Some key elements: lighting, fabric, music, and, of course, fresh flowers. Covering tables and sofas in unusual material, creating flattering lighting with candles, illuminating warm elements (like the wood paneling in this house), and strewing petals everywhere are all tricks of designers but they'll work as well for your own events. By drawing attention to these dreamlike details, a host can also hide a multitude of sins. Less-than-perfect paint, carpet, and furniture are all artfully disguised when one practices the old craft of *trompe l'oeil.*

solstice *succulents*

Two Roman deities are closely associated with the winter solstice, Saturn and Ops. We still know of Saturn, god of agriculture, because the last day of the week, Saturday, is named for him; in the old days, he represented the ending of the year. Ops, goddess of abundance, was at one time honored for eleven days in December with the wild festival of Opalia, but is hardly remembered at all now, except within the words "opal" and "opulent."

For this solstice celebration, "opalescence" is the theme, so the table holds silvery sage and blue succulents, plants that grow year-round and can thrive in almost any condition. A bit of sand supports several different varieties in a milky blown-glass compote. Particularly striking are the fleshy green or sage-colored rosettes of "hen and chicks," so called because of its tendency to naturalize and multiply in the garden. Storing water in their juicy leaves to withstand drought, most succulents come from desert or semidesert areas and need very little maintenance. It's fun to while away a winter's day at your local nursery and see which kinds strike your fancy, as you concentrate on sizes, shapes, textures, and colors. They take many different forms. One variety, stoneface, doubles here as a place-card holder.

Matte-purple grape hyacinth is a tonal accompaniment to the blue-green succulents and can often be found in late winter. For their miniature stalks, a silver toothpick urn proves to be a clever container, perfectly scaled to size. Slender tea glasses would work as well. Like narcissus varieties, grape hyacinths can survive for hours out of water. Tie a handful with ribbon or twine (mirrored fabric is used here) and put alongside place settings for an unusual accent.

st. valentine's
canopy

BLACK BARRACA,
BLACK BEAUTY, AND
BLACK MAGIC ROSES

PRIVET BERRIES

RED AMARYLLIS

What would Valentine's Day be without red roses? Actually, there are so many equally sensuous and symbolic flowers available in February, it's almost a shame to ignore them. Crimson amaryllis, deep pink tulips, plum callas, ruby red anemones, and even tiny forget-me-nots would please most people as much as or more than the often overpriced, stiff hothouse roses for sale almost everywhere right before the day. On a holiday that can be both commercial and cloying, it's exciting to expand one's notion of what evokes romance.

Nodding to tradition, 'Black Barraca', 'Black Beauty', and 'Black Magic' roses dominate this seductive twilight setting but they are a few steps away from what one might find in a typical florist bouquet. Cut short and tumbling over the edges of their Moroccan-inspired containers, these focused masses of color are offset by matte-black privet berries. Deep red amaryllis have graceful long stems, but don't be afraid to cut them down for short arrangements; gathered together, they create a sculptural, undulating surface.

Masses of torn petals are like a decadent carpet around the amaryllis and the beaded votive candleholders—imagine the unforgettable impression they'd make scattered over a fluffy comforter in a candlelit bedroom!

pitchers
full of color

HYACINTHS

KUMQUATS

RANUNCULUS

POPPIES

Bold color and high contrast were the goals in creating these masses of hyacinths and kumquats, which are mixed with a few ranunculuses and poppies for texture. The fleshy, upright stems of hyacinths also do well on their own. It's fun to experiment with new combinations of colors. Familiar shades look fresher when placed next to out-of-the-ordinary neighbors. Typically, purples are paired with pinks or whites, but this unexpected juxtaposition of purple and deep orange makes the colors "pop." Small and egglike, scattered kumquats cleverly echo the hues above without overwhelming the table surface.

Clear glass containers aren't the best choice for woody stems as the stems tend to make water murky. Heavy lusterware pitchers work here both because they easily support the weighty fruit and flowers and also because they resemble sideboard decanters. Almost any ceramic, metal, or opaque glass pitcher will achieve the same effect.

When preparing hyacinths, remember to remove the tough white section at the base of the stems for better water absorption. Note that here, there's no need for added foliage—the kumquat leaves and the hyacinth's own green spears do nicely.

A sideboard is a perfect showcase for several arrangements. When you become passionate about flower arranging, you might begin to reserve certain spaces in your home to show off

your bouquets. Or you may find yourself continuously rearranging furniture and other objects to highlight them. Fresh flowers are exquisite because they are ephemeral. And since their beauty lasts only a short time, it's fitting that we place them to their greatest advantage, even if it takes a little extra effort.

orchid *elegance*

PAPHIOPEDILUM,
CYMBIDIUM, AND
DENDROBIUM ORCHIDS

GARDENIAS

AMARYLLIS

LIMEQUAT BRANCHES

Sophisticated parties call for equally sophisticated tables. Because orchids are available year-round, they make lush displays at wintertime galas, holiday celebrations, and New Year's Eve festivities. While these once-rare flowers retain an exotic allure, they are actually quite accessible nowadays and are grown and shipped all over North America.

To complement the crystal, flatware, satin cloth, and gilded chairs of this ornate table, I chose several different types of orchids. The cool, pale greens of the *Paphiopedilum, Cymbidium,* and *Dendrobium* orchids pair well with the creamy white gardenias, amaryllis, and miniature citrus branches.

A marble compote, which provides a fullness to table arrangements, is used to showcase the amaryllis and the fruit. If your bowl is shallow, place a metal frog inside. Once you've positioned the stiffer branches, fill out the arrangement asymmetrically with amaryllis, letting the flower heads droop naturally over the edge. Looped and draped strands of pearly seed beads add a touch of opulence.

In addition to the center compote and two apothecary jars filled with *Dendrobium* sprays, an assemblage of branches and cut flowers spans almost the entire length of the table.

The central elements of this collage are lime and yellow limequat branches, the fruits of which have been "sugared" with iridescent glitter for an over-the-top effect that echoes the party's other glamorous touches. To make fruit glisten, brush one piece at a time with a thin layer of glue. Take a handful of fine glitter, sold at craft stores, and cup your hand around the fruit until it is covered. Shake off any excess when the glue dries. Single fruit globes can be rolled in glitter. Real sugar may also be used, if you prefer a matte finish.

To make your assemblage, place the branches lengthwise and position cut orchids and gardenias randomly among the fruits and leaves until you have displayed blossoms on both sides of the table. The effect can be loose and spare or dense, almost mosaiclike, depending on your taste. A silvery-white beaded placemat is used here, but the flowers can also be placed directly on a tablecloth, as long as you sponge away any excess moisture. Gardenias will last well into the evening, and orchids are even hardier, so they can live without water for at least a day. A

Paphiopedilum is tucked into each napkin ring to lend a tropical air to the setting. A smattering of votive candles in faceted glasses subtly illuminates the entire tableau.

Certain occasions really do deserve special flowers. For most dinner parties and other get-togethers, the budget and planning will focus naturally on the food; simple, unfussy arrangements make the most sense at these times. But every once in a while, extravagance is justified and really feels glorious. When stunning blossoms are available and you can afford to spend a bit more, take the leap into abundance. In winter, perhaps more than at any other time of year, everyone's senses benefit from the beauty and fragrance that only flowers provide.

winter *glossary*

AMARYLLIS

HIPPEASTRUM; AMARYLLIDACEAE

Long lasting and very dramatic, these bulb flowers are usually grown in pots. Some wintertime favorites are the 'Papillon' and 'Germa'.

AMAZON LILY

EUCHARIS; AMARYLLIDACEAE

These lilies can last for up to three weeks because of the many buds on each stem. They look like daffodils, but a bit more refined with their exquisite green throats. Their fragrance is quite strong. This flower is a crisp addition to a winter bridal bouquet, and does beautifully with amaryllis, miniature callas, and hellebores, particularly all of the *H. orientalis* varieties.

CALLA

ZANTEDESCHI; ARACEAE

Common callas, *Z. aethiopica,* have become available in the most fantastic range of colors over the last few years. Both miniature and larger varieties are attractive. They are most dramatic when clustered together so that one can look down into their beautiful throats. Careful consideration should be taken when combining callas with other flowers. Because of their shiny, smooth crispness, they look

best with a select few, such as amaryllis. Their Art Deco lines are corrupted when combined with fuzzy foliage; when in doubt, let them pose by themselves.

CAMELLIA

CAMELLIA; THEACEAE

Camellias tend to bruise easily, so buy them or cut them when the buds are still tight. The white varieties are elegant additions to dinner-party centerpieces, especially in silver or clear glass containers. If possible, try to utilize their graceful branches as well.

CITRUS

RUTACEAE

While in temperate zones one can find fruiting citrus year-round, they are essentially winter crops. Kumquats are gorgeous with orange and bright pink poppies and peach parrot tulips. Lemons are attractive with white arrangements. Tangerines make a complementary splash of color against deep plum flowers.

CYCLAMEN

CYCLAMEN; PRIMULACEAE

Though rarely seen as a cut flower, cyclamen is easily found in plant form during the winter months and does well in bouquets. Try white blossoms with miniature white callas and paperwhite narcissus.

FIR

ABIES; PINACEAE

Even if you never decorate your home for the winter holidays, bring in some fir branches to add a fresh, outdoorsy fragrance and cheerful greenery in cold months. They do best by themselves or in garlands and wreaths.

FORSYTHIA

FORSYTHIA; OLEACEAE

Forsythia is a favorite branch for forcing. In areas that freeze, it can be coaxed to bloom indoors in a matter of weeks. It takes well to tall arrangements with other green-yellow flowers, such as pale ranunculuses, daffodils, and tulips. Black or purple privet berries contrast nicely with forsythia.

FREESIA

FREESIA; IRIDACEAE

Freesias bring color as well as perfume into wintertime homes. White combines well with the ranunculuses and tulips that become available in late winter. These also look very sweet singly, tucked into tiny bottles.

GERANIUM

PELARGONIUM; GERANIACEAE

Geraniums are great houseplants to use for wintertime cuttings. My personal favorite is the fuzzy, peppermint-scented *P. tomentosum*.

GRAPE HYACINTH

MUSCARI; LILIACEAE

This miniature flower is available throughout the winter and spring and has an even more spectacular fragrance than its larger cousin. It is pretty in tiny mixed spring bouquets with green ranunculuses and snowdrops. Like other hyacinths, they make the strongest impression when clustered by themselves.

HELLEBORE

HELLEBORUS; RANUNCULACEAE

H. niger is commonly called the Christmas rose, because it blooms even in winter. It has lustrous, dark green leaves and two-inch white or greenish white flowers. Also popular are *H. orientalis* and *H. foetidus*. The greens are exquisite, and the shape of the plant is remarkable. I use them in almost all winter arrangements that call for a green, white, soft pink, or dark dusty pink element.

HYACINTH

HYACINTHUS; LILIACEAE

The deep blue-purple common hyacinth *(H. orientalis)*, with its sweet fragrance, does best by itself in masses, though a few sprigs in any arrangement add bursts of color.

NARCISSUS

NARCISSUS; AMARYLLIDACEAE

Another favorite for wintertime forcing, narcissus varieties such as paperwhites are related to the daffodil. Daffodils are single-flowered, while the rest of the tribe is complex, or multiheaded. They typically have an intoxicating fragrance and come in many creamy colors and delicate shapes.

OLIVE

OLEA EUROPAEA; OLEACEAE

Laden branches of green, purple, or near-black olives are available from late fall through spring and provide lovely draped foliage. They pair well with winter lemons and yellow, plum, and white flowers. The silvery green leaves are eye-catching but often need to be stripped quite a bit to show off the fruit.

ORCHID

ORCHIDACEAE

Exotic, diverse, and rabidly adored in almost every country and culture, with over 30,000 species and 80,000 hybrids to prove it, orchids are a top choice for opulent, sensual occasions. Because they can be cultivated indoors, wintertime provides lots of opportunities to show them off. I especially enjoy pure white *Phalaenopsis* and green-and-white *Paphiopedilum*. Many are surprisingly easy to care for as houseplants, and most survive very well as cut flowers.

bibliography

Bulfinch, Thomas.
Bulfinch's Mythology.
Modern Library Edition,
New York:
Random House,
1998.

Colette.
Flowers and Fruit.
New York:
Farrar, Straus, and Giroux,
1986.

Edwards, Carolyn McVickar.
The Return of the Light.
New York:
Marlowe and Company,
2000.

Eliot, T. S.
Four Quartets,
"Little Gidding."
New York:
Harcourt, Brace and World,
1943.

Page and Gold, eds.
Botanica.
New York:
Welcome Rain Publisher Llc,
1999.

Pritchard, Tom, and Jarecki, Billy.
Trade Secrets.
New York:
Clarkson N. Potter, Inc.,
1994.

Sackville-West. Vita.
The Joy of Gardening.
London:
Amereon, Ltd.,
1992.

Sunset Western Gardening Book.
Menlo Park, California:
Sunset Publishing Corporation,
1994.

Walker, Barbara.
*The Woman's Encyclopedia
of Myths and Secrets.*
San Francisco:
Harper and Row,
1983.

Yenser, Stephen.
The Fire in All Things.
Baton Rouge:
Louisiana State University Press,
1993.

acknowledgments

FROM ARIELLA

This book would not have been possible without the support, time, and love of the amazing people who have helped me along the way. I owe thanks for the possibility of this book to the ever lovely Christina Wilson. Thanks also to Leslie Jonath, for feeling that my perceptions of color and the natural world might interest others and for transforming that into the reality of this book. To Elise Cannon, for arranging your words so beautifully and for translating mine with such grace. Your patience and affection have filled my heart. To Shaun Sullivan, for capturing magic. Your keen eye for beauty and your talent for portraying it have depicted the flowers on these pages in their best light. To Jodi Davis, for all your hard work. To Vivien Sung, for your vision. To Anthony Albertus, for repeatedly assembling the most perfect additions to my last-minute inspirations. I am so grateful for all the treasures you procured and for your encouraging, calming nature. To Simonetje, Renaissance damsel that you are, for working out colors with me. To Maneena Douglas and Simone, for making the world's most beautiful marzipan peaches. To Sarah Silvey, for coming up with such a hilarious and creative use for "butt plants." You are a treasure! To Joseph, for being there always. To Georgene, Serena, Wenonah, and Erin, artists and lovelies all. To Gabriel, for everything you have taught me. To Diane, for your incredible wisdom and love. To Tamaré, for your lifelong friendship. To Walter, for the beauty that always surrounds you; your devotion to your art has always inspired me. To Gayla, for your generosity of spirit. Your way with flowers awes and inspires me. To Cindy, for your enthusiasm and love. To Brian, for your humor and friendship. To Sara, for your support and encouragement. Thanks to everyone at the San Francisco Market for procuring the beautiful elements that grace these pages. To Gloria Sullivan, for opening your house to us. To Emily and Isabel Sullivan, for your valuable help. To Vicky and Valerie, foragers extraordinaire. To Kaye Heafey, for allowing us to photograph your stunning grounds. To Murray Rosen, for all the lovely cuttings. To Deborah Bishop, for the use of your Moroccan treasures. To Dan Ziegler, for the use of your incredible home. To Hellie Robertson, for letting us shoot in and around your beautiful house and gardens. To Manu, for soothing me through the agony. Your calmness and love sustains me.

FROM ELISE

Many thanks to my mother, Minette Blanchet Davison, for teaching me to love flowers. To Ariella, for your generosity and vision. Thanks also to Leslie Jonath and Jodi Davis of Chronicle Books, for making it all happen; to Sharilyn Hovind, for her expertise; to David Knupp and Michael Ruggiero, for their comfort; and to all my friends at PGW. And especially, gratitude and love to Dr. Susan Raeburn, for her kindness, support, and wisdom.

resources

NOTES

ABC CARPET AND HOME
881 & 888 Broadway at
E. 19th Street
New York, NY 10003
212.473.3000
www.abchome.com
Vast selection of accoutrements
for the home.

ANTHROPOLOGIE
Stores nationwide and catalog.
800.309.2500
www.anthropologie.com
Tabletop, linens,
home accessories.

ARIA
1522 Grant Street
San Francisco, CA 94133
415.433.0219
Antique garden and architectural
ornament, lighting, and furniture.

THE AVANT GARDENER
1460 Marine Drive
Vancouver, B.C. V7T 1B7
604.926.8784
Garden-inspired items.

BANANA REPUBLIC HOME
Stores throughout North America.
888.906.2800
www.bananarepublic.com
Tableware, linen,
home accessories.

BELL'OOCCHIO
8 Brady Street
San Francisco, CA 94103
415.864.4048
Fabric, ribbons, millinery supplies.

BOTANICA
1633 West Lewis Street
San Diego, CA 94702
619.294.3100
Stylish floral design, smart,
chic accessories.

**BOTANIX— LES GRANDS
JARDINS DE LAVAL**
2900 Boulevard Labelle
Chomedy-Laval, Quebec
H7P 5S8
450.682.9768
450.682.9513
Fine floral items.

BRITEX FABRICS
146 Geary Street
San Francisco, CA 94108
415.392.2910
www.britexfabrics.com
Large selection of fabrics
from around the world.

CALVIN KLEIN HOME
Stores worldwide.
800.294.7978
Tableware, linens,
home accessories.

CAMPO DE FIORI
Route 7
Sheffield, MA 01257
413.528.1857
www.campodefiori.com
Fantastic selection of garden
and home accessories.

CHALK HILL CLEMATIS
P.O. Box 1847
Healdsburg, CA 95448
707.433.8963
www.chalkhillclematis.com
Incredible selection of specialty
cut flowers as well as clematis
nursery. National shippers of both.

CHELSEA GARDEN CENTER
250 West 9th Avenue
New York, NY 10011
212.929.2477
www.chelseagardencenter.com
Large selection of containers,
plants, and flowers.

CHINTZ & CO
1720 Store St.
Victoria, BC V8W1V5
250.388.0996
www.chintz.com
Floral fabrics and accessories.

COST PLUS
Stores worldwide.
800.COST.PLUS
www.costplus.com
Home furnishings and
accessories from
around the world.

CRATE & BARREL
Stores nationwide and catalog.
800.967.6696
www.crateandbarrel.com
Home furnishings and
accessories.

DAY GROW GREENHOUSES
RR No. 5, Baker Road
Saskatoon, Saskatchewan
S7K 3J8
306.374.4022
Flowers and garden supplies.

THE GARDENER
1836 4th Street
Berkeley, CA 94710
510.548.4545
www.thegardener.com
Garden merchandise,
vases, and accessories.

GARDEN HOME
1799D Fourth Street
Berkeley, CA 94710
510.559.7050
Topiary, orchids, accessories
inspired by the garden.

THE GARDEN TRELLIS
8015 Maple Street
New Orleans, LA 70118
504.861.1953
Plants, flowers, and containers.

HOBBS
2129 West 41st Avenue
Vancouver, British Columbia
V6M 1Z6
604.261.5998
Garden accessories and
tableware.

KACKENHOFF NURSERIES LTD.
P.O. Box 2000
St. Norbert, Manitoba
R3V 1L4
204.269.1377
Flowers and garden supplies.

MAISON D'ETRE
92 South Park Street
San Francisco, CA 94107
415.357.1747
Magical selection of antique
and contemporary treasures
for the home.

PIER ONE IMPORTS
Stores nationwide.
800.245.4595
Candles, vases, tableware.

**PINKS: A GIFT SHOP
FOR GARDENERS**
4235 Dunbar Street
Vancouver, BC V6S 2G1
604.222.3772
Floral-inspired gifts.

PORTICO
72 Spring Street
New York, NY 10012
212.941.7800
Eclectic furnishings, art,
home textiles, and
decorative accessories.

POTTERY BARN
Stores nationwide and catalog.
800.922.5507
www.potterybarn.com
Attractive, affordable furniture
and accessories.

RESTORATION HARDWARE
Stores nationwide and catalog.
800.762.1005
www.restorationhardware.com
Home accessories and furniture.

SMITH & HAWKEN
Stores nationwide and catalog.
800.776.3336
www.smithandhawken.com
Floral accessories, furniture,
books, etc.

SUMMER HOUSE
1833 4th Street
Berkeley, CA 94710
510.549.9914
Vintage goods and fine
home accessories.

SUR LA TABLE
Stores nationwide and catalog.
800.243.0852
www.surlatable.com
Everything you could want
for the kitchen and table.

**TAIL OF THE YAK
TRADING COMPANY**
2632 Ashby Avenue
Berkeley, CA 94705
510.841.9891
Exquisite glassware,
fine papers, ribbons, etc.

TAKASHIMAYA
693 5th Avenue
New York, NY 10022
212.350.0100
800.753.2038
Exquisite tableware and
home accessories.

THE UNIQUE FLORIST
467 Broad Street North
Regina, Saskatchewan
S4R 2X8
306.789.1010
Flowers and floral accessories.

ZOHRA FABRICS
235 West 40th Street
New York, NY 10018
212.719.9617
Beautiful selection of silks
and other fine fabrics.

index

. . . every thing that grows
Holds in perfection but a little moment . . .

—WILLIAM SHAKESPEARE, SONNET 15